1. US Rangers move in to assist a Parachute Regiment soldier 'kill' his billowing parachute (a US Irvin type rather than a British GQ) during a joint unit jump in Washington State.

UNIFORMS ILLUSTRATED No 10

The PARAS

THE BRITISH PARACHUTE REGIMENT

JAMES G. SHORTT

ARMS AND ARMOUR PRESS

Introduction

ablished in 1985 by Arms and Armour Press
6 Hampstead High Street, London NW3 1QQ.

istributed in the United States by
erling Publishing Co. Inc., 2 Park Avenue,
ew York, N.Y. 10016.

ritish Library Cataloguing in Publication Data:
hortt, James G.
he Paras: The British Parachute Regiment. –
  Uniforms illustrated; no. 10)
  Great Britain. *Army. Parachute Regiment* –
istory   2. Great Britain. *Army* – Equipment –
istory
  Title   II. Series
56'.166   UA652.P3
BN 0-85368-699-8

diting, design and artwork by Roger Chesneau.
ypesetting by Typesetters (Birmingham) Ltd.
rinted and bound in Italy.
y Tipolitografia G. Canale & C. S.p.A. - Turin
  association with Keats European Ltd.

The Parachute Regiment shares a common point of origin with both the Commando movement and the Special Forces that developed out of the Second World War – more specifically, the vision of Dudley Clarke that led to the formation of the Commandos and subsequently the Paras, the SBS and the SAS. All these élite forces have the twin tasks of dealing with the 'hottest' problems in any war and of handling the difficulties of internal security in peacetime.

During the Second World War, British airborne troops spearheaded operations in North Africa, France, Sicily, Italy, the Low Countries, Germany, Greece and the Far East, and in more recent years the Paras have been pitched against terrorists in Palestine, Malaya, Cyprus, Aden and Northern Ireland. Their friendly operations have included duties in Jordan, the Trucial States and Anguilla, where their presence restored the rule of law, whilst some of their finest hours have been experienced at Suez, in Borneo and in the Falklands. They have deployed by air, land and sea, and their orbit extends from policing to conventional and special operations. Furthermore, the British Parachute Regiment tradition has been the starting point for many other countries' parachute formations, including those of France, Belgium, the Netherlands, Canada, the United States, India and Pakistan.

Behind the fighting men of the Parachute Regiment is their tenacious logistical support – artillerymen, engineers, medics, and signals, transport, ordnance, workshop and attached personnel, from PTIs to catering and ecclesiastical, all wearing the maroon beret (that Paras often claim makes them bullet-proof!). The Paras have now once again been brigaded as airborne in the recently revamped 5th Airborne Brigade with its out-of-area responsibilities as Britain's troubleshooters.

As a former Para, I should like to thank the Parachute Regimental Association (of which I am a member) for its assistance, and especially Maj. G. Norton (ret) and Mr. T. H. Fitch BEM, curator and custodian respectively of the Airborne Forces Museum at RHQ, The Parachute Regiment, Browning Barracks, Aldershot; all photographs reproduced here are by courtesy of The Parachute Regiment and the Airborne Forces Museum. Finally, I should like to dedicate this book to the British Para past, present and future.

James G. Shortt

◀2
. A Scimitar CVR(T) – Combat Vehicle Reconnaissance (Tracked) – with its 30mm Rarden gun is
rewed by members of 1 Para Recce Troop during a
lizzard in Norway. The Parachute Regiment now
as its own light armoured capability. Note the cold-
eather protective ski masks worn by the commander
nd radio operator.

▲3

3. Sir John Dill (Chief of the Imperial General Staff), swagger stick in hand, inspects a drop container and parachute at Tatton Park in December 1940. The previous June, Prime Minister Winston Churchill had suggested that General Dill form a corps of at least 5,000 parachute troops, as an airborne arm of the commando or special service units being formed. Next to General Dill, pointing at the container, is the commanding officer of No. 2 Commando, Lt. Col. I. A. Jackson. No. 2 Cdo. was designated for parachute

training – Special Air Service, as it was then called – from November 1940.

4. Members of the newly formed 11th Special Air Service Battalion receive final briefing before boarding an Armstrong Whitworth Whitley Mk. V prior to jumping at the Central Landing School, RAF Ringway, near Manchester. All parachutists can be seen wearing the black pilot's helmet, issue battledress, and the Parachute Type 'X' Equipment designed by the GQ company.

▼4

5. Parachute-commandos of 'X' troop, 11th SAS Battalion, prior to their engagement in the first British airborne operation – a commando raid to destroy the Tragino aqueduct in southern Italy under the name 'Operation Colossus', 9 February 1941.
6. Easily mistaken for the enemy, parachutists of 11 SAS assemble outside a hangar at RAF Ringway. They are wearing the earliest

British airborne helmet, made of rubber and nicknamed 'rubber bungee' by the paratroops. They are also wearing the khaki brown parachute smock adapted from the German Fallschirmjäger combat smock. Two paras can be seen to wear respirator haversacks on their chests over the 'X' harness of their parachutes.

▲7 ▼8

. Using an adapted children's slide, parachutists are taught how to perfect the 'landing and roll' technique, coached by RAF instructors at Ringway. The trainees are all wearing battledress and the issue 'ammunition boots'. Behind the training apparatus can be seen parachutes stacked in racks. This photograph was taken prior to the re-formation of 11 SAS as the 1st Parachute Battalion in September 1941.

. Early experiments with camouflaged parachutes were carried out at Tatton Park, the drop zone for RAF Ringway. These parachutists can also be seen to be testing the new rimless parachutist's steel combat helmet. The helmet was based on one captured from the Germans during the invasion of Belgium.

. Two Wehrmacht prisoners are searched by men of 'C' company, 2nd Parachute Battalion, following their capture during a raid to seize radar equipment at Bruneval in France, 27–28 February 1942. Note the early British airborne smocks and steel para helmets. One para carries an SMLE No. 3 Mk. 1 and a German Mauser Gewehr 98.

10. On board a naval motor gunboat following the Bruneval raid, members of the 2nd Parachute Battalion explain how they 'liberated' a German army helmet to an RAF wing commander. Visible are SMLE Mk. 3 rifles (one with a 1907-pattern sword-bayonet attached), a Sten gun and items of 1937-pattern webbing equipment.

9▲   10▼

11. Maj. J. D. Frost, OC 'C' Company, 2nd Parachute Battalion, wearing airborne steel helmet and smock, discusses the Bruneval raid with a lieutenant-colonel from the Parachute Brigade. The lieutenant-colonel from the Grenadier Guards is wearing the badge of the airborne division – Bellerophon brandishing a spear and mounted on the winged horse Pegasus. This badge, designed by Edward Seago and worn on both shoulders of the battledress did not become standard wear for parachutists all ranks until May 1942.

12. Bruneval raiders glad to be 'back in Blighty' as the naval gunboat that took them from the French coast after the action docks in Britain. As well as the airborne helmets and smocks, two men can be seen wearing their parachute qualification wings on their right shoulders. One parachutist has obtained a souvenir of the raid – a German steel helmet.

13. Volunteers for the Parachute Regiment (as it became in August 1942) are trained in how to release themselves from the harness of their type 'X' parachutes whilst undergoing selection. As can be seen from the variety of headdress and badges, they are drawn from many different regiments. Parachute Regiment instructors visible in airborne smocks are still wearing their parent regiment badges with a dark blue beret; later they would receive the badge of the Army Air Corps, of which the Parachute Regiment became a part.

14. Parachute Regiment recruits at RAF Ringway in August 1942 are subjected to an air-sickness test under medical supervision by being laid on a stretcher suspended by ropes and swung back and forth for twenty minutes. Note that the RAMC lieutenant wears parachute wings.

▲11   ▼12

▲15 ▼16

15. Members of the Royal Welch Fusiliers undergo training at RAF Ringway prior to designation as the 6th Parachute Battalion. Note the modified, rubber-lined parachutist's training helmet that superseded the 'rubber bungee'. The man nearest the camera has recorded his name, training initiation date and number of jumps (six to date) on the rim of the protective helmet. August 1942.

16. In October 1941 the 50th Indian Parachute Brigade was formed from Indian, Gurkha and British units, and the first air landing school being established at Willingdon airport, New Delhi. Here, recruits undergo improvised ground training at Willingdon. The 50th Indian Parachute Brigade later formed the basis for the 1st and 2nd Indian Parachute Regiments.

17. The first two recruits to the Indian Parachute school show their sand-coloured airborne smocks and type 'X' parachutes, October 1941.

18. An RAF instructor at RAF Chaklala (whither the Indian parachute training centre moved from New Delhi), adjusts and checks the parachutes of British, Gurkha and Indian parachute recruits before they embark on board a Dakota aircraft. Note that some trainees are wearing balaclavas padded with rubber sheeting as an improvised parachute protective helmet. October 1942.

17▲ 18▼

▲19   ▼20

19. Troops from the 151st (British) Parachute Battalion (50th Indian Parachute Brigade) at RAF Chaklala. These men, under RAF instruction in November 1942, wear woollen pullovers instead of smocks and all can be seen wearing the airborne helmets improvised from balaclavas and rubber sheeting.

20. British paras from 5 Company, 1 Para, after their capture in the Tamera Valley, north of Beja in Tunisia, by Fallschirmjäger ('German paras). In addition to airborne helmets, some are wearing the Denison smock which, along with the maroon beret was introduced in time for Operation 'Torch', the invasion of North Africa in November 1942.

21. In preparation for the invasion of Sicily, further parachute brigades were raised, and ad hoc training was carried out in North Africa prior to July 1943. Here, under the scrutiny of a member of the Army Physical Training Corps, members of the Parachute Regiment, with members of the 2nd Special Air Service Regiment, Long Range Desert Group and No 1 Demolition Squadron ('Popski's Private Army'), undergo training in doorway exit drills from a Dakota.

22. A parachute training platform constructed from scaffolding by APTC staff in Tunisia, July 1942.

▲23 ▼24

16

. Members of the 11th Parachute Battalion, in company with
me naval parachutists, don smocks, parachutes and helmets at
. 4 Parachute Training school at Kabrit in the Middle East prior
a training jump. Note the rubber-strip protective knee pads and
d-style smocks.
. Parachute troops wearing knee protectors, helmets and para-
utes climb in to a Wellington bomber converted for parachute
ining, November 1943. Note the exit port under the fuselage
ar the tail wheel and the desert boots worn by these men at Kabrit.

25. General Dwight Eisenhower, Commander-in-Chief during
Operation 'Torch', inspects a parade of British parachutists in May
1943. The paras are wearing their maroon berets with Army Air
Corps badge which earned them the name 'Red Devils' in North
Africa. They are dressed in khaki drill bush jackets and shorts, the
latter referred to by the troops as 'Bombay bloomers'.
26. A bayonet charge through a smokescreen as paras train for
Operation 'Husky', the invasion of Sicily in July 1943. The weapons
are the new SMLE No. 4 with spike ('pig sticker') bayonets.

26▼

▲27 ▼28

27. Training for 'Husky', a para throws a grenade, having first put down his Sten Mk. 2. Note the length of toggle rope attached to his 1937-pattern webbing equipment. Each paratrooper carried such a length.

28. Covered by his 'oppo', a paratrooper prepares to fire a PIAT at a designated target during training for Operation 'Husky'. The Projector Infantry Anti-Tank weapon could throw a 3lb grenade a distance of 100yds.

29. A Parachute Regiment mortar crew sight in on a target as they prepare to fire a British 3in mortar. The mortar, which weighed 124lb, was dropped with the paras in a container and could throw a 10lb bomb a distance of 1,600yds.

30. Parachute Regiment gunners firing a US 75mm M8 pack howitzer. The M8, although starting life as a mule pack weapon, became the pre-eminent airborne artillery piece for both British and US formations because of its small size and easy manoeuvrability.

▲31 ▼32

31. With the invasion of Sicily under way, paratroops of the 6th Airborne Division are back in Britain training for the invasion of Europe, July 1943. Here, a paratrooper unloads his 98cc Welbike from a CLE round container while his 'mate' tries one out.

32. HM King George VI meets the Parachute Regiment and is shown a weapons valise which is attached to the parachutist by a line so that it can be lowered beneath him when his canopy deploys.

33. A paratroop machine gun section from the same parade at Aldershot. This crew has a water-cooled .303 Vickers machine gun, which saw service in the British Army continuously from 1912 to 1960. On the ground can be seen the tripod on which the weapon was mounted. One of the crew holding a Sten Mk. 2 sub-machine gun wears the special-issue multiple magazine pouches and has also padded his left shoulder strap with foam.

33▶

. In preparation for
'̶verlord' (the invasion
̶ northern France in
̶44), this paratrooper
̶s been equipped with
̶mall drum which
̶ntains carrier pigeons
̶ relay messages in the
̶sence of radio com-
̶unication. Note the
̶rachute wings on the
̶enison smock.

. Paratroops in their
̶d berets and wearing
̶e new parachute
̶giment badge designed
̶ May 1943 group with
̶der troops to touch a
̶egasus' soft toy mascot
̶r good luck prior to
̶verlord'. The para-
̶oper holding the
̶ascot carries a Sten
̶k. V sub-machine gun
̶ross his chest.

. Easily identified by
̶eir berets and Para-
̶ute Regiment badges,
̶ese men gather to
̶eck each other's para-
̶ute harnesses. It
̶ould be noted that
̶ey are wearing the
̶ive drab sleeveless
̶arachutist's smock over
̶rly-pattern sleeveless
̶enison smocks.

. Paratroops prepare
̶ spearhead 'Overlord'
̶ advance of 'Neptune'
̶y silencing the German
̶astal defence batteries
̶ Melville: members of
̶Para with attached
̶aff talk to their pilots
̶fore departure at
̶wn, June 1944. The
̶eration had to start 30
̶inutes before the main
̶ndings.

̶34

35 ▲

36 ▲   37 ▼

▲38

38. Members of the Parachute Regiment board their aircraft in the morning of 6 June 1944. All wear sleeveless airborne smocks on top of their Denison smocks, and the centre paratrooper (whose face is obscured by a censor's mark) has a Fairbairn-Sykes fighting knife hanging from his webbing.

39. Further elements of the 6th Airborne Division climb into a Whitley prior to departure for France in June 1944.

40. A member of the Parachute Regiment kitted out for HALO (High-Altitude Low-Opening) operations. He wears the SAS pre-DPM camouflaged windproof smock and trousers with puttees and DMS boots. Between his legs is slung an 'A' frame canvas bergen which, when his canopy is deployed, can be lowered so as not to entangle his legs on landing. His parachute is a GQ model with reserve on which is mounted an altimeter and oxygen gauge. He is just attaching his oxygen mask to his helmet, and his L1A1 rifle is secured at his left side.

▼39   40▶

41. An RAF parachute instructor checks personal equipment before a jump. This equipment is carried in the personal kit container between the parachutist's legs, and after the jump the container is lowered beneath him before landing. The parachutist is wearing the old-style steel airborne helmet little changed in design since the Second World War, a later-pattern Denison smock and olive drab cotton lightweights with DMS boots and puttees. The nets are for safety, one being allocated to each man.

42. A Parachute Regiment soldier about to fire a Vigilant anti-tank guided missile. This para, in standard red beret, Denison smock lightweights and 1958-pattern webbing, holds the Vigilant sight control unit; beside him is the missile in its launch container. The Vigilant is a first-generation, wire-guided anti-tank missile developed by British Aerospace and, being man-portable, is an effective addition to the Parachute Regiment's armoury. It can penetrate up to 550mm of armour plate.

43. The three-man crew of an 81mm L16 medium mortar prepare to fire their weapon. The green squares identify them as members of 3 Para; 1 Para uses a red square and 2 Para a blue square. The soldier in the centre is holding the bomb, which weighs just under 4½kg; with this weapon the mortar team can put down white phosphorus smoke or high explosive rounds. The mortar is designed to break down into three one-man loads and is parachuted in by container. These paras are wearing camouflaged face veils as cravats.

◀41

42▲ 43▼

▲44　▼45

44. 3 Para march towards their start-line for the assault on Mount Longdon. The rugged hill country shows the type of terrain the troops had to traverse with personal equipment often weighing in excess of 100lb.

45. Mount Longdon, stormed by 3 Para and on which Sgt. Ian McKay died; he was later awarded the Victoria Cross. The track running across the picture is the width of a Land Rover and gives an idea of scale. This photograph was taken at first light after the battle.

46. Sgt. R. H. Mayhew of 8 Para receives the Military Medal from General Montgomery. Note that the General is wearing the Parachute Regiment badge next to his General's beret badge, whilst on his shoulder is the formation sign of the 21st Army Group. Sgt. Mayhew wears the parachute title, red on a yellow field, above his wings.

47. General Montgomery, the Commander-in-Chief, pictured with senior officers and the commander of the 6th Airborne Division. All wear red berets, and the officer in the third row directly behind the General wears the Canadian Parachute wings first authorized in September 1943.

46▲ 47▼

▲48

▲49 ▼50

48. Operation 'Market Garden' in September 1944 (better known as Arnhem), when the 1st Allied Airborne Army of British, Polish and US airborne units set off for Holland from 24 British airfields. Here, members of the Parachute Regiment don the sleeveless airborne smocks over their Denison smocks and webbing so that their parachute harnesses will not become entangled with their web equipment.

49. British Parachute Regiment officers stand in front of the US markings on a Dakota prior to emplaning for 'Market Garden'. Note the different methods in which pistols are carried: the officer on the left uses a closed-top holster behind his right magazine pouch; the officer in the centre wears an open-top holster on the belt on his left hip; and the latter's companion wears his closed-top holster low on the right hip. Note also the despatch rider gauntlets that became popular with Parachute Regiment officers.

50. Airborne gunners load a Willys jeep towing a 6pdr anti-tank gun; the gunners shield would be removed prior to embarkation on board the Horsa glider seen in the background. The 6pdr was developed in 1938 (but not produced until 1942), and the weapon was later adopted by US airborne forces as their 57mm Gun Mk. 1.

51. Defenders of Arnhem. Pictured here are members of 1 Platoon, 21 Independent Parachute Company, with two glider pilots on the Arnhem perimeter near the Stationsweg. The photograph was taken on 22 September 1944, and standing from left to right are the two pilots; Sgt. Binnick (with head veil); Pte. Gillespie; Pte. McCausland; Pte. Cameron (died of wounds at Arnhem); and Cpl. Rodley (killed the next day). Kneeling are Sgt. Swallow (died of wounds at Apeldoorn on 13 December) and Sniper Pte. Jeffreys.

52. Preparing for the German attack on their position, British paras at Arnhem take cover in a shell hole, weapons cocked and ready to fire.

51▲   52▼

▲53

▲54 ▼55

. British paratroops
ken prisoner by the
ermans are inter-
gated by an officer. A
erman guard wears his
mouflaged poncho as a
mbat smock.
. Members of the
rachute Regiment,
any of them wounded,
e marched into
ptivity by the Germans
ter the fall of Arnhem
27 September 1944.
. Paratroops'of 4 Para
epare to emplane at
indisi on 12 October
44 for Operation
Ianna', the airborne
ndings in Greece
articularly the libera-
on of Athens). Note the
akotas used as the
opping aircraft.
. Elements of 4 Para
nd at Megara airfield
ar Athens in stage one
Operation 'Manna'.
cause of strong winds,
er 40 paratroops were
jured in the landings.
. Wearing Union Jack
mbands so that they
ll not be mistaken by
rtisans as Axis troops,
e paras advance on
thens from Megara
rfield.

56 ▲   57 ▼

58. Taking cover from allies: a British para shelters from sniper fire directed by the Greek partisans of ELAS (Ellinikos Laikos Apeleftherotikon), who resented the British presence. Behind the para can be seen a British tank. December 1944.

59. Signpost for the future: British paras involved in internal security operations against ELAS guerrillas search a suspect in an Athens street.

▲58 ▼59

0. Members of 5 Para
ake cover during house-
learing in Athens
gainst ELAS,
December 1944. Note
he M1A1 carbine in .30
alibre, a semi-automatic
weapon that had a pistol
rip and folding butt for
JS airborne use. The
ara wielding the
weapon also carries wire-
utters on his belt order
ebbing; beside him is a
ren gunner and behind
im a para with the .45
hompson M1 sub-
nachine gun, a selective
re weapon.
1. Pte. Blacknell, a
niper with 5 Para, takes
over in the Acropolis
verlooking Athens and
vaits for ELAS guerillas
o abandon the burning
uilding in the centre,
December 1944.

▲62

63▶

62. 2 Platoon of 5 Para
man a Bren gun against
ELAS guerrillas on the
Acropolis in Athens.
The officer with the field
glasses, a parachute
major, directs fire.
63. A mortar section of 5
Para brings 3in fire to
bear on ELAS guerrillas
from the Parthenon.

64▲

◀65

64. A Vickers .303 machine gun is directed against ELAS fighters by British paratroops who have stormed and seized the KKE (Kommouni-stikon Komma Ellados – Greek Communist Party) building in Constitution Square, Athens.

65. Wearing white camouflaged smocks and trousers, members of a recce patrol of 'B' Company, 9 Para, scout out an area of the Ardennes, January 1945.

66. A British paratroop officer from the 6th Airborne Division interrogates a German prisoner near Wesel in Germany after the crossing of the Rhine in March 1945. The German wears the Iron Cross and also what appears to be a Luftwaffe breast badge, but the collar and epaulette insignia are army wear.

67. British paras inspect the body of a Nazi guerrilla of the SS 'Werewolf' organization killed during a sabotage operation, April 1945. His body is on display where it fell, along with a notice in German to discourage other 'Werewolves'.

68. The Commander-in-Chief (India), Sir Claude Auchinleck inspects men of 15 Para. Note that on their pegasus badge they have the inscription 'India' and that their parachute qualification wings are worn on the right breast. The men wear No. 6 warm weather parade dress. 15 Para was formed from Chindit units as part of the 44th Indian Airborne Division.

69. Gurkhas emplane for the 'Dracula' operation in Dakotas assisted by the RAF crew. A kukri (Gurkha knife) is just visible under the parachute harness of the leading man.

▲66 ▼67

70. Three Gurkha lieutenants from the 2nd and 3rd Indian Parachute Regiments receive the Distinguished Service Medal from General Wavell in the presence of Brigadier Hope-Thompson. Note that, here, parachute wings are worn on the right shoulder. Both the lieutenant-colonel and the brigadier wear the 'light bulb' parachute badge denoting airborne troops, on a slouch hat.

71. CO Lt. Col. Whyte with his staff of the 7th Indian Parachute Field Ambulance in September 1945. From August 1945, men of this unit carried out the last combat jumps of the war, entering prisoner-of-war camps in Thailand, Java and Singapore, to give aid to captives. Note the 44th Indian Parachute Division patches, pegasus with 'India', and jump wings on the right breast.

72. Singapore, 1945: the war over, these members of the 5th Parachute Brigade have been deployed as Provost staff. The windshield of the Willys jeep carries the legend 'Airborne Provost' and Pegasus insignia, so there can be no doubt as to their origin. In addition to their red berets (and in the case of the driver and one other man, their Parachute Regiment badges), the men wear the airborne patch on the shoulders of their bush jackets and the red and yellow parachute regiment titles used with this type of uniform. The jeep, fresh from war service, carries no number plate, only the designation number '79'.

73. In Cyprus, EOKA (Ethniki Organosis Kyprion Agoniston – National Organization of Cypriot Fighters), a group created in 1953, started a military campaign in April 1955 through sniping, street murder, arson and bombing, to drive the British out of Cyprus. Here, a Parachute Regiment corporal of 16 Independent Parachute Brigade stands guard with a dog handler of the Royal Military Police. The RMP handler wears the original camouflage-pattern windproof which the SAS adopted during ski training in Lebanon during the Second World War; the para wears the conventional Denison smock and 1944-pattern belt, and carries a Sterling sub-machine gun (the L2A1 introduced in 1954).

72▲　73▼

41

▲74

74. Parachute Regiment soldiers detain EOKA suspects within the stockade of a British military base in Cyprus. The corporal in the centre of the photograph is armed with a Sten Mk. 5 sub-machine gun, a 9mm selective fire weapon. He has a toggle rope on his 1944-pattern web belt kit and his companion, though apparently armed only with a stave, has a revolver attached to a lanyard in his trouser pocket.

75. EOKA suspects are turned around for ID purposes under the supervision of an officer. Note the revolver on the left side with lanyard to left shoulder for cross draw – the approved IS method of

▼75

the time. The webbing and holster are 1944-pattern.

76. RQMS 'Chirpy' Robinson assists Pte. J. Morrison of 'S' Company, 3 Para, on 5 November 1956 prior to Operation 'Musketeer', when the battalion dropped on Port Said, Suez, during the Anglo-French operation against Egypt. Note the Denison smocks, steel parachutist's helmet and olive green lightweight trousers of cotton drill. The RQMS wears 1937-pattern web anklets, whereas Pte. Morrison wears puttees. The rubber-soled ankle boot seen here replaced the leather-soled 'ammunition' boot.

76▶

77. A member of 3 Para stands rooftop guard over a devastated Port Said. He carries a 7.62mm Simonov SKS rifle liberated from the Egyptians, and around his waist is a bandolier of ammunition. The SKS, made in the Soviet Union, first put in an appearance in 1945 and became the standard export weapon to Soviet-style regimes until the advent of the AK47.

78. Job done, but ordered out by politics, members of 3 Para are ferried from shore to ship for the journey back to Cyprus, having handed over to UN troops. The 1944-pattern equipment, along with the 'A' frame canvas bergens, can be seen amongst the personal equipment.

79. Argentines captured by 3 Para during their advance on Port Stanley are disarmed and searched. Notice that each soldier carries a 66mm section anti-tank rocket (L1A1 HEAT); the paras at Goose Green and Darwin used these weapons to clear Argentine bunkers and trenches.

80. The Band of the Parachute Regiment greets members of 2 and 3 Para on their arrival back at RAF Brize Norton, the parachute training school, following the Argentine surrender.

▲77　▼78

81. The Colonel Commandant, Sir Anthony Farrar-Hockley, with the Colonel-in-Chief of the Parachute Regiment, HRH Prince Charles, greets the commanding officers of both Parachute battalions. Note that the Prince wears the wings and red beret that he won through selection, in the same way as any Parachute Regiment soldier.

82. Desert-pattern DPM parachutist's smock trousers and parachute helmet cover developed from the normal temperate- and tropical-pattern DPM used by British forces. This equipment is currently being developed with a view to it being available to Parachute Regiment troops should 5 Airborne Brigade's role ever demand it.

83. A para peers around a tree. He is wearing DPM arctic-issue smock and trousers, with Northern Ireland-issue gloves.

. The latest GQ Parachute in DPM (Disruptive
[Pa]ttern Material), designated for Special Forces and
[Pa]rachute Regiment special operations and path-
[fin]der activity, and available from 1985.

. King Hussein listens to Brigadier Gordon of 16
[In]dependent Para Brigade as elements of the brigade
[pa]rticipate in a joint exercise with the Jordanian Arab
[Le]gion, July 1958. The exercises were a cover to
[in]sert the paras in support of King Hussein who,
[du]ring an Iraqi invasion and subversion from
[N]asser's United Arab Republic, had asked Prime
[M]inister Macmillan for military aid. The Brigadier
[ha]s donned his maroon beret immediately upon land-
[in]g; deflated parachutes can be seen behind him.

. Troopers make their way through the rough and
[ro]cky terrain of the Hashemite kingdom by jeep,
[ha]ving been parachuted in from the Suez Canal zone.
[So]me men have wound camouflaged veils around
[th]eir berets.

84

85▲   86▼

87. Though withdrawn in November 1958, the British presence undoubtedly deterred action by Iraqi and UA troops, who still remembered the paras' aggressive fighting at Port Said two years earlier. Here paras scal a rocky hillside to rendezvous with an Ara Legion patrol. They ar still armed with .303 Brens and SMLE No. 4s, which would soon b replaced by FN 7.62 FALs (later SLR, L1A and MAGs (GPMG). Many of the paras wear veils, benouse style, around their berets.

88. Elements of 'C' Company, 1 Para, train in amphibious landing: from LCUs (Landing Craft Utility) operated by the Landing Craft Wing of the Royal Marine Commandos, early 1960s. Clearly to be seen is the new 1958 pattern webbing with i tell-tale 'Y' yoke. The troops are in shirtsleev order and may be oper ing off Cyprus.

▲87 ▼88

Members of 'B'
...mpany, 3 Para,
...ched to 45 Com-
...ndo Royal Marine as
...t of Radforce in May
...4. The role of
...dforce, working with
...roop, 'A' Squadron,
...2 SAS, was to pacify
...Radfan mountains in
...rthern Aden where
...yptian and Yemeni
...versives were trying
...lunge the Arabian
...insula in to a 'war of
...ration'. Here, the
...as prepare to move
..., having been landed
...a Royal Navy
...copter giving
...stical support to the
...al Marines. Note the
...s of disintegrating-
...7.62mm ammuni-
... for the GPMG
...ed out amongst the
...ol; note also the
...ence of large packs
... bergens. The soldier
...he immediate fore-
...nd has extra water,
...cessity in the
...fan, with a 1944-
...ern water-bottle
...ier attached to his
...8-pattern webbing.
...Cautiously, Lt. Col.
...sh, CO 3 Para, lifts
...head above the line of
...otective stone sangar
...ng operations in the
...fan, May 1964. The
...eibi tribesman of the
... were notoriously
...d snipers, and were
...osed to the British
...inistration.

89▲   90▼

91. A member of 3 Para and a Royal Marine of Commando patrol through Aden city, 1965. Note that both wear the skeleton-order belt kit of two 1958-pattern pouches, and note also the difference in issue between the para's khaki wool shirt and the light cotton shirt. Both men are armed with the L1A1 rifle.

92. Members of 1 Para prepare for a patrol in Aden. Note the use of both long- and short-wheelbase Land Rover in camouflage; these a traditionally stripped down, with windshield and doors removed – hence the use of sand goggles. The steel spa the front of the Land Rover prevents cables strung across the road from decapitating or injuring the crew. Th Aden command sign visible on the front of vehicle.

▲91 ▼92

93. A Sergeant
Instructor at the Para-
chute Regiment depot at
Aldershot displays the
firepower available to the
British soldier. Note that
he wears the short-lived
V necked jumper that
was at one time issued
for working dress. Start-
ing nearest the camera,
the weapons shown are
an 84mm Carl Gustav
M2 rocket launcher; a
9mm Browning HP S/A
pistol; a 7.62mm GPMG
with feed box; a 7.62mm
GPMG for the sustained
fire role; 38mm signal
pistols; a No. 36 defen-
sive hand grenade and an
L1A1 Grenade, Rifle,
Anti-Tank; an L2A3
Sterling 9mm sub-
machine gun; a 51mm
mortar; and an L1A1
SLR 7.62mm.
94. A mortar platoon of
3 Para disembarks from
Sir Geraint at
Thessalonika, Greece,
during Exercise
'Olympic Express' in
August 1969; 3 Para
would again meet Sir
Geraint, a Royal Fleet
Auxiliary, in the
Falklands conflict. The
lead men have L2A3
9mm SMGs and
personal field dressing
taped to the harnesses of
their 1958-pattern
webbing.

93▲   94▼

▲95   ▼96

In March 1969
itish paratroops were
shed to the Caribbean
and of Anguilla to
store law and order.
e job done, they
nded over to seconded
icers of the London
etropolitan Police in
ptember 1969. This
ra corporal carries an
' frame bergen and his
uty frees' while
dding farewell to the
cals, and one of his
ccessors, at the airstrip
rimeter.

. Paratroops climb
oard an RAF Hercules
craft for the return
ght from Anguilla to
itain in September
69.

. L/Cpl. Shawe of 'A'
ompany demonstrates
other use for his
herry beret' when
oseiling on the cliffs of
enhale in November
69.

. Paras lent a helping
and in Malta after an oil
nker ran aground in
ovember 1969. Here,
en of 'B' Company, 3
ara, form a human
ain to get a line to
rvivors and assist the
altese police with
sualties. Note the life
eservers worn by those
the surf.

99. HRH the Duke of Edinburgh reviews the US Army parachute display team during a visit by the latter to the Parachute Regiment's 'Red Devil' Free-Fall Display Team. Note that the Americans have been awarded their maroon berets and parachute regiment badges.

100. Maj. Peter Schofield, team commander of the 'Red Devils', makes an exit from an aircraft over the Great Yorkshire Show at Harrogate. The 'Red Devils' team travels round Britain promoting parachuting and the Parachute Regiment. Note that Maj. Schofield has a smoke grenade attached to his ankle and that he is using a small microphone to enable him to communicate with the ground and with the aircraft.

101. Members of the Parachute Regiment undergo training in HALO (High-Altitude Low-Opening) techniques where a static line is not used. They wear oxygen masks because of the height of the aircraft and are attached to a central respirator with individual gauges prior to switching over to individual cylinders situated on top of their reserve. Interestingly, the paras are wearing old-style, SAS-pattern windproof camouflaged smocks and trousers instead of Denison smocks. It was the SAS who pioneered HALO techniques amongst the British military.

102. HALO jumpers of the Parachute Regiment prepare to exit out of the rear cargo door of a Hercules aircraft of the Royal Air Force. The jumpers are wearing GQ Aeromair chutes.

101 ▲   102 ▼

▲103 ▼104

3. Members of the Parachute Regiment training in
e Trucial States. Here, a gunner loads a Wombat
– a 120mm calibre Battalion Anti-Tank weapon
th an M8 .5in spotting rifle on top. The BAT is
mouflaged for the desert, but the stripped-down
ng-wheelbase Land Rovers in the background are
ished in the desert pink pioneered by the SAS
ring their experience in Oman. Note that these
ras wear the khaki peaked fatigue cap made
pular in this part of the world by the SAS.
4. A group of paras seeks the advice of a local
besman in Bahrain. The photograph brings to
ind the quip often heard in para and commando
cles: 'The most dangerous thing in the world is an
ficer with a map!'
5. Paras wearing the blue beret with the badge of
e UNICYP (United Nations Intervention Forces in
prus): Force Commander Gen. Prem Chand
eaks with Acting Drum Sergeant Major Cornish
ring a parade in which the former presented UN
rvice medals to the paras for their work in Cyprus.
ote that Sgt. Maj. Cornish wears the white warm-
eather ceremonial uniform tunic with red NCO sash
ross his right shoulder and his drum major sash
th Parachute Regiment battle honours across his
ft. He holds a Parachute Regiment drum major's
ace in his right hand, and note the wire-
mbroidered ceremonial wings and bandsman drum
ove the stripes.
6. Members of 7 RHA wearing the necessary body
mour (a fragmentation vest) wait in a Belfast side
reet for a call to action. Note that at least two
ldiers have their wooden riot batons pushed in the
mhole of the fragmentation vest. Normally the unit
ves artillery support to the Parachute Regiment,
t in Northern Ireland the men act as foot soldiers
ring their tours of duty.

105▲   106▼

107. Pte. Pablo James and Star. With developments in Northern Ireland, a number of new internal security tactics were introduced, the major theme being policing and Military Aid to the Civil Powers as opposed to a military counter-insurgency campaign. One of the results was the introduction of dog handlers to the Parachute Regiment for guard and police duties, particularly at HMP Maze (Long Kesh prison).

108. L/Cpl. Ingram of the Regimental Provost staff, Para, on 'lollipop' duty outside Springfield Road RUC station. Taped to his 1958-pattern belt is an individual field dressing.

109. 2 Para embark on board HMS *Intrepid*, a Royal Navy assault ship used for commando operations. The date is 27 July 1972 and the troops are leaving Portland for a tour of duty in Belfast. It should be noted that they carry the fragmentation vest body armour, which has just been issued to them on leaving mainland Britain.

110. A mobile patrol of 'B' Company, 2 Para, in autumn 1972. The patrol have made their Parachute Regiment badges tactical by darkening them, and the soldier in the left has his S6 respirator in a 1944-pattern water-bottle carrier. Rifle slings are not attached to the front sling swivel of the L1A1s they carry. The Land Rover, a long-wheelbase model, has been stripped of its side doors.

▲107 ▼108

109▲ 110▼

▲111   ▼112

11. Back in Aldershot, the car-bombing of the Officers' Mess of the 16th Parachute Brigade by Official IRA terrorists on 23 February 1972 was in revenge for the action of 1 Para in Derry the previous January (called 'Bloody Sunday' by the IRA). The explosion killed the Parachute Regiment's Roman Catholic chaplain and six civilian staff. The photograph shows Paras from all branches of the Brigade clearing debris in order to reach survivors.

12. 'B' Company, 2 Para, take a tea break in Duncairn Gardens, Belfast, in the summer of 1972. Two of the patrol favour Denison smocks whilst the other two wear the newly issued DPM (Disruptive Pattern Material) combat smock under their fragmentation vests. The paras' L1A1 rifles are fixed to their wrists by the loops of the rifle slings.

13. CSM Adams and Maj. Wilde of Support Company, 3 Para, in Borneo in May 1975, while attending the jungle warfare school in Brunei. They wear olive drab tropical combat dress. Maj. Wilde sits on his butyl-laminate patrol bergen, near him his belt order with 'golok' (jungle knife) and L1A1 minus sling; CSM Adams wears an OD jungle hat and on his wrist an MoD-issue watch with its grey safety strap. Interestingly, Maj. Wilde is wearing DMS boots and puttees instead of jungle boots.

14. A Depot instructor tries to encourage a Parachute Regiment recruit during 'P' company selection in a log race on Heart Break Hill, Aldershot. Until he has passed this gruelling test of stamina and teamwork the recruit is not allowed into the Parachute Regiment family. Note the numbered, old-style olive drab working dress and steel para helmet.

113▲   114▼

63

15. Members of 'B' Company, 3rd Battalion Parachute Regiment, debus from an armoured personnel carrier (APC) fitted with a recoilless gun during exercises in Germany in August 1979.

16. A Parachute Regiment medic applies a first field dressing to a simulated leg wound suffered by an 'enemy soldier' during BAOR exercises in July 1978.

17. Soldiers of the Parachute Regiment handling a Milan missile launcher from the back of a Land Rover under simulated NBC conditions at the Infantry Trials and Development Unit of the School of Infantry in 1980.

18. A Small Arms School corps instructor familiarizes a Parachute Regiment soldier with the Milan missile launcher at the Infantry Trials and Development Unit.

117▲ 118▼

▲119 ▼120

119. Members of 'A' Company, 1 Para, in 1982, showing the new parachutist's smock in DPM with ribbed cuffs and stud-fastening pockets. The garment i based loosely on the old Denison smock which i replaced.

120. Members of 2 Company, 10 Para (a T. unit), with Russian weapons – an AK47 (7.62mm × 39mm) and an PRD LMG in the same calibre – during training with instructor of 21 SAS (also a TA unit). The para with the AK47 wears German parachute qualification wings over his right breast pocket.

121. 2 Para is ferried from Fitzroy to Bluff Cove on 4 June 1982 by LCU advance parties of 2 Para, now under 5 Brigade instead of 3 Commando Brigade, who had already moved forward by helicopter and seized the settlement. The troops, who are wearing foul-weathe gear over their clothing are the veterans of the battles of Darwin and Goose Green at which their CO, Col. H. Jones won the Victoria Cross.

122. Lt. Col. H. Jones vc, CO of 2 Para, who was killed leading his men to victory in the first land battle of the Falklands campaign.

123. Sgt. Ian McKay vc killed on Mount Longdon clearing a machine gun position during 3 Para's assault and capture of the feature during the 1982 South Atlantic campaign.

121▲ 122▼

 123▼

124. Soldiers of 1 Para attached to AMF (Allied Command Europe Mobile Force) on exercises in Norway during January–March 1984. They are wearing arctic white camouflage over DPM arctic smocks and have camouflaged their weapons with white tape.

125. Members of 1 Para on AMF duties in Norway refer to their map for guidance during a cross-country ski-ing exercise.

126. A 1 Para general-purpose machine gunner, covered by his 'oppo', lies up in deep snow awaiting contact with the 'enemy' during AMF exercises in Norway, winter 1984

127. Michael Heseltine, Secretary of State for Defence, visited the Headquarters of 5 Brigade on 14 November 1983 to mark the official granting of the title 'Airborne' to the unit; he is seen here inspecting an airborne guard of honour which includes Gurkhas, Army Air Corps troops and Parachute Logistic troops amongst Parachute Regiment members.

124▶

▼125

▲128 ▼129

70

8. Following the re-establish-
ment of 5 Brigade as 'Airborne',
members of 2 and 3 Para were
flown to Fort Lewis,
Washington, to exercise with
elements of the 2/75th Airborne
Rangers who had led the Joint
Caribbean and US Task Force
Operation against Cuban troops
at Port Salines Airport,
Grenada, on 25 October 1983.
Here, Parachute Regiment
soldiers meet members of the
Rangers. Both units have an
out-of-area responsibility.

9. Washington State, USA:
members of the Parachute
Regiment and 2/75 Airborne
Rangers wait to emplane aboard
Lockheed C-5A and C-130
transports.

0. Members of the Parachute
Regiment acting as Warsaw
Pact or 'Orange' forces deploy
from C-130 Hercules over
Germany during the autumn
'84 'Lionheart' exercises.

1. Having landed, an
'Orange' force Parachute
Regiment soldier collects his kit
from his container and prepares
to group with his comrades and
put distance between him and
the drop zone. A 66mm LAW
tube can be seen across his
back.

130▲ 131▼

71

132. A Parachute Regiment officer of the 'Orange' forces communicates with BAT HQ during 'Lionheart' He wears the wings of a Army Parachute Jump Instructor (APJI).

133. Moving through German farmland, 'Orange' force Parachute Regiment soldiers advance to make contact with 'Blue' forces during Exercise 'Lionheart', autumn 1984. Note that the radio operator is carrying only a Sterling SMG for personal protection.

▲132 ▼133